Is A Life of Wellness Possible
And
How Do You Achieve it?

A Study from God's Word To Take You Into
A Life of Healing and Health

by

Ann Windsor
New Life School of Pneumatology
New Life International Apostolic Ministry
211 S. College Street
Lincoln, IL 62656
annwindsor8@gmail.com

Father, I pray for every person who will use this book. I pray that you will give them eyes to see, ears to hear and hearts to understand what the Spirit is saying to them.

I pray that they will take this book personally, for their own health and well being. I know that You watch over Your Word to perform it. Thank you for bodies healed and even souls saved in the lives of those reading herein.

If you don't know Jesus as your Savior, He is ready to give you forgiveness and a new life in Him. Pray this simple prayer:

"Jesus, I believe that you died for my sins and rose again having gained my forgiveness. I receive the sacrifice that You made for me on the Cross, and I receive You into my life as my Savior. Teach me to know You, to listen to You and to follow You. I want to be Your disciple. Thank You for saving me,

In Jesus' Name, Amen."

(About the cover: "Corpus Hypercubus" by Salvador Dali.)

Is A Life Of Wellness Possible?

Table of Contents

3) God chastens with sickness
4) Paul's thorn
5) Paul's eye condition
6) "If it be Thy will"

Is A Life of Wellness Possible & How Do You Achieve It?

Introduction:

There are three views of divine healing: first, that it passed away; second, that it is a special grace; and third, that healing is in Redemption. The following is a short summary of the three views:

Passed away: Healing was a gift given to the apostles to attest to the validity of the gospel.

Special grace: given only to <u>some</u> who need healing. Rejects the view that healing was included in the plan of redemption.

A part of the Work of the Cross in Redemption: therefore it belongs to every believer.

This study is based on the third view, that healing and health are a part of Redemption.

The Word - The Example - The Work of the Cross

Feed - Do Not Just Read

written scripture
final authority
~ not try - but trust
~ 1st Relationship

FIRST: THE WORD OF GOD

The basic doctrines of all mainline Christian denominations usually begin with this statement:

> The Scriptures, both the Old and New Testaments, are verbally inspired of God and are the revelation of God to man, the infallible, authoritative rule of faith and conduct. (Assembly of God)
>
> The original autographs of the sixty six books which make up the Bible are considered to have been divinely inspired, by which it is meant that they are infallible and authoritative. Reference to the scriptures is made in settling every religious question. A pronouncement from the scripture is considered the final word. The basic textbook of the church and the basis for all preaching is the Bible. (Church of Christ)
>
> We believe in the plenary inspiration of the Holy Scriptures, by which we understand the 66 books of the Old and New Testaments, given by divine inspiration, in-errantly revealing the will of God concerning us in all things necessary to our

salvation, so that whatever is not contained therein is not to be enjoined as an article of faith. (Nazarene)

The Holy Bible was written by men divinely inspired and is God's revelation of Himself to man. It is a perfect treasure of divine instruction. It has God for its author, salvation for its end, and truth, without any mixture of error, for its matter. Therefore, all Scripture is totally true and trustworthy. It reveals the principles by which God judges us, and therefore is, and will remain to the end of the world, the true center of Christian union, and the supreme standard by which all human conduct, creeds, and religious opinions should be tried. All Scripture is a testimony to Christ, who is Himself the focus of divine revelation. (Southern Baptist)

At times Jesus would start his encounters with people by asking them a question, so that would be a good place to start.

Is the basis of faith for healing, experience or "What Is Written"?

The Written Scriptures must be our final authority to settled all matters of faith and practice regarding divine or supernatural healing.

We are told to "study to show ourselves approved unto God", (2 Timothy 2:15).

What are we to study? The Written Word of God, with what we study from that Word becoming our final authority for faith and practice, rather than man's interpretation or opinion.

In the book of Genesis, God revealed Himself as a Healer. Healing is seen throughout the Old Testament and we are living under a new and better covenant in the New

Testament. Remember, we have the SAME GOD as the Israelites had.

The Old Testament, "I am the Lord, I change not", (Malachi 3:6), is the same as the New Testament Jesus Christ, Who is the "same, yesterday, today and forever," (Hebrews 13:8).

In Matthew 6:33, we are taught to believe God will meet our material provisions today, as He did for Israel, so why do we 'cut off' believing Him to heal our physical bodies as He did the Israelites?

Hosea 4:6: "My people are destroyed for lack of knowledge."

There is no teaching on this subject in many places, or the teaching there is states that healing was only to establish the Church in the beginning, and now the day of healing (miracles) is over.

This is why we must absolutely go to the Word of God itself as our Final Authority, especially regarding healing for our physical bodies.

SECOND: THE MINISTRY OF JESUS

What was the first foundation for total confidence regarding God's willingness to heal you? His Written Word.

"Who" establishes a <u>correct</u> <u>interpretation</u> of the Written Word?

Jesus: His example and His teaching. *THE WILL OF GOD IN ACTION + word*

Hebrews 1:3 tells you that Jesus was the embodiment of God to us. God spoke to man through prophets in the Old Testament. Now in the New Testament, He actually came among us in the Person of His Son.

9

Jesus was *the <u>will</u> of God* in word and action among us, and
Jesus <u>was</u> *God* in Action among us.

Jesus' example should be the yardstick by which we judge any interpretation of or teaching from the scriptures.

As we look at the Gospels, was there anyone Jesus ever refused to heal?

Even in the book of Acts, healing was a continuous operation of God through the Church and we see various forms of healing in Acts that we did not see in the gospels, yet they were God-approved methods of ministering healing. We will look at these as we go along.

You must see clearly in your mind the example of Jesus regarding healing of people's physical bodies.

Your faith cannot be confident unless it is firmly based upon God's written Word, **and** the Person of Jesus Christ, His words and His works.

Tradition makes the Word of God of none effect and gives a form of godliness, but without power.

We must resurrect a cry that was heard in the church in the mid-19th century: "BACK TO JESUS"....the Healing Jesus.

Jesus' example is the Force behind the Written Document which states "by His Stripes you are healed", (Isaiah 53:5).

Jesus willingly healed BEFORE the stripes were laid on His back for our healing. He healed those who came to Him based upon His Compassion:

"Jesus went forth and saw a great multitude, and was moved with compassion toward them and healed their sick", (Matthew 14:14).

Now, through the Work of the Cross, healing is based in Redemptive, legal reality. Everything Jesus did while He was on earth, is now available on legal grounds. and is available to all who call upon Him in faith, Romans 4:16:

"So the promise is received by faith.
It is given as a free gift."

Healing is based in COMPASSION and COVENANT (New Testament).

When the devil argues with the Written Covenant, take him back to the Compassionate Example: Jesus.

THIRD: THE WORK OF THE CROSS

Isaiah and Peter both included the words, 'by his stripes you are or were healed' in their writings. Does this mean physical healing? If it does, can you appropriate healing like you do forgiveness? To be healed you must be convinced that your physical healing is just as much a part of the work of the Cross as forgiveness for your sin. We are going to looked at the two passages in Isaiah and Peter, the words and their meanings in Hebrew and Greek and lay a foundation for your healing that ties directly to Jesus' suffering and death for you.

For you needing healing: healing does not have to be a difficult thing to understand and believe. There is a lot of information in this workbook, and you don't need to know and use all of it to be healed. A little knowledge of these three foundations, acted upon, is sufficient for you to be healed:

TRINITY / final authority

The Written Word — 4 gospels = all healed
Jesus' Example
The Work of the Cross

TO BE HEALED, YOU MUST BE CONVINCED
Accept the authority within the
4 GOSPELS

"IT IS WRITTEN" — J's final say on any matter

Where did sickness, disease and death begin?

Satan, the Adversary

Where does sickness come from? Does God make people sick? Did He create the world with sickness in it? Is God putting or allowing this sickness to ravage my body and life? We will look at all these questions, but first let's begin with where sickness and disease originated. The Bible points clearly to Satan as the fountain from which all of mankind's troubles spring.

The Bible describes Satan to have been perfect in the day that God created him. He was known then as Lucifer, son of the morning.

Isaiah 14:12: "How you are fallen from heaven, O Lucifer, son of the morning."
Ezekiel 28:15: "You were perfect in all your ways from the day you were created until iniquity was found **in** you."

Lucifer fell in his heart before he fell from heaven. He was no longer of a perfect heart but his foolish heart was darkened, and changed into the image and nature of sin. Spiritual death was the result. Spiritual death being separation from God AND a change of nature.

Lucifer's name was changed to Satan, the Adversary of God. When God created man and woman in His image, Satan became our adversary, for he hates and opposes all that God loves and creates.

The Commission

When God created man, he was given a job to dress and keep the garden, Genesis 2:15:
"And the Lord God took the man and put him into the garden of Eden to dress and to keep it."

In Hebrew these words mean:
dress...to protect, guard.
keep...to tend.

Why would God instruct him to 'guard' something if there _wasn't an enemy_?

The Warning

Now, think about **the warning** and how it was stated in Genesis 2:17: "But of the tree of the knowledge of good and evil you shall not eat, for in the day you eat thereof you shall surely die."

In Hebrew, which is the language the Old Testament was written in, this word is really a plural: 'deaths'.
Or, "in dying (spiritually) you shall die (physically)".

Did Adam and Eve die physically when they ate of the tree of knowledge? No.

Eating of this tree resulted in their going from a nature of innocence to a sinful nature and separation from God. The change in them was immediate. When God came to walk with them in the cool of the day, they hid themselves, ashamed of their nakedness. And the blame-game began.

Immediate spiritual death resulted in physical death 930 years later, "And all the days that Adam lives were nine hundred thirty and he died", (Genesis 5:5).

Paul understood this great truth and states it in his letter to the Romans, Chapter 5, Verse 12: "by one man, Adam, sin came into the world and death by sin, and so death passed upon all mankind."

Another way of saying of that verse is: "Through Adam's sin, a door was opened. Spiritual death and physical death came through that door and attacked all mankind."

(image from ddmgaragedoors.com)

Remember, this word 'death' is plural: Spiritual and physical. Sickness is 'baby death'.

Sickness

Physical sickness was not part of God's original creation.
Physical sickness can be defined as 'incipient death'.
Incipient: embryonic, beginning, budding.

Or we could say: physical sickness is the beginning, the bud of death. or, 'baby death'. Death in its infant form.

Sickness when it grows up results in death.

If spiritual death had not entered this world through Satan gaining the advantage of Adam and Eve, we would not have physical death or sickness in its many forms today, just as we would not have sin in its many forms.

Sin and sickness are Siamese twins.
They are two sides of the same coin.

Sin brought sickness and death with it into the world.

In Genesis 3, God uses the word 'curse' to describe the effect of Adam & Eve's disobedience: "cursed is the ground (or a curse had been loosed upon the earth) because of what you have done," (Vs. 17).

Just as he is the originator of sin, Satan is also the originator of sickness. He is also works in every generation to spread it throughout the human race. The Bible tells us that he has special evil spirits whose chief business it is to make people sick.

> Luke 13:11: "behold, a woman had a spirit of infirmity eighteen years and was bowed together and could in no wise lift up herself."

> Luke 13:16: "ought not this woman, whom satan hath bound these eighteen years, be loosed from this bond?"

The word 'infirmity' here is: astheneia.
Greek meaning 'sickness'.

The New Testament was written in the Greek language. Astheneia is the commonest word in the Greek language for sickness. This woman had a **spirit of sickness**.

Plainly the Scriptures tell us that sin, sickness and death did not originate with God, but with Satan.

Satan tempted Adam and Eve and they didn't 'guard' the garden.

Through Adam sin, sickness and death was loosed into this world.

Now it works every day at attacking people everywhere.

God did not create this problem, but because He loves us, He took responsibility for providing a solution.

God is not the author or originator of sin, sickness and death.

He is the Answer for it!

Concluding this section:

Where did sin originate? In the heart of Lucifer.
What was Lucifer's name change to? Satan.
What does the name Satan mean? Adversary
What was the state of the earth and mankind when we were created? Perfect.
What job did God give us? To guard and keep our 'gardens'. (Your life is *your* garden.)
Why the need for guarding? Because God was forewarning us that there was an Adversary on the loose.
What was the warning God gave to Adam and Eve? To not eat of the Tree of Knowledge.
They ate of that tree anyway.
What as the result? The same as Lucifer experienced. They experienced spiritual death…..separation from God.
Spiritual death then produced what? Physical death.

According to Paul in Romans 5:12, sin opened what? A door.
What came through that door? Death.
What had its beginnings in sin and spiritual death being loosed upon the world? Sickness and physical death.
What is sickness?
The beginning of physical death, (baby death!)

God called this sickness and death what? A curse.
What has He done to deal with this curse?
Provided the Answer through the Cross.

For you needing healing: please think these things through until you can get it settled that God is not the author of the sickness that you are dealing with.

There can be no sure faith for healing if you are doubtful about this.

If you need to discuss this further, contact me at my email: annwindsor8@gmail.com.

God's Will and Physical Wellness

Sickness and disease is a part of the present world through the sin of Adam. As humans, we are delivered into a groaning creation when we are born. Sickness and disease were not part of God's original intention for mankind or this world.

The word 'redeem' means to **buy back**. God took on the responsibility of redeeming us so that we could, as His people, enjoy our lives as He originally planned it to be.

1 Peter 1:18-19:
Forasmuch as you know that you were not redeemed with corruptible things, such as silver and gold; But with the precious blood of Christ, as of a lamb without blemish and without spot.

....God paid a ransom to save you. (TLB)

This redemption was for your whole being: inward and outward. When Jesus was on earth, He demonstrated what the redeemed life was like: He healed the sick, the brokenhearted, and set free the demon-possessed.

He said: "I came not to do my own will, but **to do the will of Him Who sent me**", (John 6:38). What Jesus did was God's will. Healing the sick was a major part of His ministry.

Jesus did not act independently of the Father. The Father's power **on** Him, **in** Him and **through** Him was what brought healing and deliverance to the captives.

The Father's power is His Presence, His life, His being. His virtue, anointing, power, and ability;

Luke 5:17:
"And the power of the Lord was present to heal,"

Acts 10:38:
"How God anointed Jesus of Nazareth with the Holy Ghost and with power: who went about doing good, and healing all that were **oppressed of the devil**; for God was with him."

This verse from Acts gives the New Testament understanding of the continued source of sickness and disease, the devil. We can see this truth running through the entire Bible about the source of mankind's troubles.

Calamities are not 'acts of God' as insurance companies and religious tradition claim. Did Jesus ever cause calamities?

Everything Jesus did, every good act, and gracious word, was the Father in Him doing it. It was God's will to heal all that came to Jesus for healing.

In the book of Acts, we see God at work through the Body of Christ doing the same things that He did through His Son.

Restored to wellness

God created mankind to live in wellness.
Through sin, that life of wellness was lost.
Jesus came to redeem us from the 'lost-life' into the life of wellness.

Jesus' Body and His Blood represent the 'buying back to wholeness', the redeeming of our entire being.

Really look at these scriptures:

1 Thessalonians 5:23
"And the very God of peace sanctify you wholly; and I pray God your whole spirit and soul and body be preserved blameless unto the coming of our Lord Jesus Christ."

......May the God of peace himself make you entirely pure and devoted to God; and may your spirit and soul and body be kept strong and blameless until that day when our Lord Jesus Christ comes back again.   (The Living Bible)

3 John 2
"Beloved, I wish above all things that you may prosper and be in health, even as your soul prospers."

Dear friend, I am praying that all is well with you and that your body is as healthy as I know your soul is!   (TLB)

For those of you needing healing: take these verses personally.   When Paul or John says, "I pray your", or "Beloved", put yourself into those statements.

Think, really think about the example of Jesus if you are questioning God's willingness to heal you.   Did Jesus ever refuse to heal anyone who came to him?

Do you read in the book of Acts that anyone was refused healing?

Be encouraged, Jesus Christ is the same, yesterday, today and forever!

TWO SCRIPTURES FROM THE WORD OF GOD FOR WELLNESS

There are three foundations for healing and wellness: the Word of God, the Example of Jesus, and the Work of the Cross.

We will look now at TWO Scriptures that, if thoroughly studied and understood, will uphold you as you are receiving your healing.

Word Definitions

Why study definitions?

William Barclay said:
"The more I study words, the more I am convinced of their basic importance. On the meaning of words everything depends. No one can build up a theology without a clear definition of the words which are to be used in it. Christian belief and action both depend upon a clear understanding of the meaning of words."

Verse 1:

> **Isaiah 53:5**
> But He was wounded for our transgressions, He was bruised for our iniquities; The chastisement for our peace was upon Him, And by His stripes we **_are healed_**. (NKJV)

Verse 2:

> ### 1 Peter 2:24
> Who Himself bore our sins in His own body on the tree, that we, having died to sins, might live for righteousness--by whose stripes you **_were_** **healed**.
> (NKJV)

The verse here quoted by Peter was originally spoken by the prophet Isaiah concerning the Messiah Jesus 750 years before He was born.

Here, I want to take a little time and actually look at the meaning of these words in their original languages. It is easy for me to say that they mean physical healing, but unless you see for yourself the proof of it, the devil can talk you out of it when you are dealing with symptoms in your body.

Isaiah wrote in Hebrew.

The word for 'healed' in Hebrew was: 'Rapha' pronounced 'raw-faw'.
For verification see this word under its listing in the Strong's Exhaustive Concordance, (you can look it up on the internet). This is the Hebrew word #7495.

This word 'rapha' was a part of the Name that God gave to Israel when He brought them out of Egypt, revealing Himself to them as their Healer. He said,

"I am the LORD, who heals you," (Exodus 15:26).

The words, 'who heals you', is 'rapha' in the Hebrew language. 'I am the Lord' is 'Jehovah'. Put together we get a compound name for God: Jehovah Rapha, the Lord your healer.

Looking at definitions of 'rapha':

to mend (by stitching),
(cause to) heal,
physician,
repair thoroughly,
make whole.
(figuratively) to cure

This particular Hebrew word was always used in reference to physical healing except once and there it was used in reference to repairing the temple altar.

In 1 Peter 2:24, Peter wrote in the Greek language and the word was: 'iaomai', pronounced 'ee-ah'-om-ahee'.

In Strong's it is #2390 and means:

to cure (<u>literal</u> or figurative),
to heal or make whole.

The one difference between Isaiah and Peter is the **_tense_** of the verb.

Isaiah says, 'by his stripes you ARE healed'.
Peter says, 'by his stripes you WERE healed'.

Peter is quoting Isaiah AFTER the death, burial and resurrection of Jesus, after the Finished Work of the Cross.

The Hebrew word in Isaiah 53:5 and the Greek word in 1 Peter 2:24 has the same meaning, and that word, in both, means _physical healing_.

Knowing this will greatly strengthen _your faith_ regarding God's will to heal.

For extra study:

In Isaiah 53:4, a context verse for Isaiah 53:5, the words 'griefs' and 'sorrows' are used.

In the Hebrew these words are referring to physical sicknesses and pains, rather than emotions:

"Surely he (Christ) hath borne our griefs (kholee, sicknesses) and carried our sorrows (makob, pains).

Let's look at the Hebrew words for each and other references where they are used:

"Kholee": sickness, from chalah, to be weak, sick or afflicted. See Deuteronomy 7:15, "The Lord will take away from thee all sickness (kholee). See also, Deuteronomy 28:61; 1 Kings 17:17; 2 Kings 1:2, 2 Kings 8:8.

"Makob" is translated, 'pain' in Job 33:19 and Jeremiah 51:8.

Isaiah 53:4, should read, "Surely he (Christ) hath borne our sicknesses and carried our pains."

T.J. McCrossen in his book, Bodily Healing in the Atonement, said, "Every unprejudiced Hebrew scholar must admit that this is the correct translation."

Now looking at the phrase, "Himself 'bore' our sicknesses".

Nasa: Hebrew, to bear in the sense of *suffering punishment* for someone else. In Isaiah 53:12 this word is also used meaning, Jesus 'bore' (nasa) our sins.

Again, McCrossen says: "All admit Christ bore our sins, but an unprejudiced mind will also admit that the Hebrew verbs indicate he also bore our sicknesses. This is very clear and there can be no other conclusion."

Sabal: Hebrew, to *bear something as a penalty or chastisement*.

How did Christ bear our iniquities? As our Substitute.

How did Jesus 'bare' and 'carry' our sicknesses and pains? How is it that 'by His stripes we are healed'?

"He who knew no sin was made to be sin," 2 Corinthians 5:21.

Note that it says, 'sin', not 'sins'.
Yes, Jesus carried away your 'sins', but He also took care of the nature that caused those sins. The sinful nature, or the nature that **made** you a sinner.

He went clear back to the cause of sin and death: the nature of sin that Adam loosed in this world, (Romans 5:12). When He cured the **root**, He also cured the **fruit**. Now we can have a life triumphant over sin as well as a life of wellness.

Young's translation: "Surely our sicknesses he <u>hath born</u> and our pains he <u>hath carried</u> them."

Commentator Alexander McLaren says of these verses:

"It is to be kept in view, that the griefs, which the Servant (Christ) is here described as bearing are literally sicknesses, and that similarly, the sorrows may be diseases. Matthew in his quotation of this verse (Mt. 8:17) takes the words to refer to bodily ailments. The Hebrew thought drew no such sharp line of distinction between diseases of the body and those of the soul. Of these two words expressing the Servant's taking their burden on His shoulders (nasa and sabal) the former implies not only the taking of it, but the bearing of it away; and the latter emphasizes the weight of the load." (T.J. McCrossen "Bodily Healing in the Atonement")

These two verses are powerful convincers when the words are looked at in the language of the writers.

****

Let's also not forget, the example of Jesus in interpreting these two verses. Matthew quotes Isaiah when speaking of Jesus healing those who came to Him.

Matthew 8:16-17:
"When the even was come, they brought unto him many that were possessed with devils: and he cast out the spirits with his word and healed all that were sick: that it might be fulfilled which was spoken by Isaiah the prophet saying, HIMSELF TOOK OUR INFIRMITIES AND BARE OUR SICKNESSES."

Here, the gospel writer specifically interprets the Isaiah 53:5 verse as applying to the healing of physical infirmities.

Jesus Healing The Sick by Heinrich Hofmann

Something to think about:

When John 3:16 is read in context, Jesus pairs it with a verse from the Old Testament that told of the Israelites being physically healed after being bitten by poisonous serpents.

John 3:14-17 (NKJV)

And as Moses lifted up the serpent in the wilderness, even so must the Son of Man be lifted up, 15. that whoever believes in Him should not perish but have eternal life. 16. For God so loved the world that He gave His only begotten Son, that whoever believes in Him should not perish but have everlasting life. 17. For God did not send His Son into the world to condemn the world, but that the world through Him might be saved.

Numbers 21:4-9

Then they journeyed from Mount Hor by the Way of the Red Sea, to go around the land of Edom; and the soul of the people became very discouraged on the way. 5. And the people spoke against God and against Moses: "Why have you brought us up out of Egypt to die in the wilderness? For there is no food and no water, and our soul loathes this worthless bread." 6. So the Lord sent fiery serpents among the people, and they bit the people; and many of the people of Israel died. 7. Therefore the people came to Moses, and said, "We have sinned, for we have spoken against the Lord and against you; pray to the Lord that He take away the serpents from us." So Moses prayed for the people. 8. Then the Lord said to Moses, "Make a fiery serpent, and set it on a pole; and it shall be that everyone who is bitten, when he looks at it, shall live." 9. So Moses made a bronze serpent, and put it on a pole; and so it was, if a serpent had bitten anyone, when he looked at the bronze serpent, he lived.

The people were not saved spiritually....there was no 'spiritual' salvation until Jesus died on the cross. This is definitely referring to physical healing.

John 3:16 is usually thought of as pertaining to spiritual salvation, but in it's larger context and the Old Testament example that Jesus used, physical healing was the context of the Old Testament verses.

Interesting??????

The Importance of Taking the Scriptures Personally

James 1:6-8 says that a double minded person receives nothing from the Lord.

What is 'double mindedness'?

It is the inward attitude of faith at one time and then doubt the next. This is a battle that we all face in receiving the promises of God.

It isn't that God is off and on about blessing you, that He is double minded. No.

It is because double mindedness constantly 'opens and closes' the receiving channel. God is transmitting, but we are turning the receiver off and on!

We turn the receiver off because the devil challenges the Written Word in our minds as he did Eve: "Has God said?" Double mindedness is inner confusion and God is not the author of confusion, 1 Corinthians 14:33:

> "For God is not the author of confusion, but of peace,
> as in all churches of the saints."

If Satan is *unsuccessful* in making you doubt God's Word about His willingness to heal, then he will work on making you doubt that God is willing to heal *YOU*.

That is when you defeat him by taking the Written Covenant (Scripture) as your personal guide to wellness with fresh determination.

Ask yourself: "Now what does **'MY'** Written Covenant say again? (New Testament means New Covenant)
Answer: "It says Jesus, Himself, took _my_ sicknesses and bore _my_ infirmities and by His Stripes, _I_ am healed."

When we are sharing the gospel with an unsaved person, many times we tell them, "if you had been the only person in the world, Jesus would have come and died for you". We personalize it just for them.

How do we reassured _ourselves_ that we were saved? We take the verses that pertain to being saved and make them personal. Here is another, Romans 10:13:

> "For whosoever (that means me) shall call upon
> the Name of the Lord shall be saved."

Now you must take the same approach with healing, making it personal for yourself.

Just as you go to the verses concerning what is written about salvation to reassure your confidence about your Father concerning your salvation, you go to the verses that are written about healing, to reassure your confidence about your stand with the Father concerning being healed. Your knowledge of the salvation verses keeps the Spirit of salvation flowing in you, keeping you saved.

Your knowledge of the healing verses and of Jesus ministry to the sick, keeps the Spirit of healing flowing in you, keeping you healed.

Yes, you can have a life of wellness!
The Spirit of salvation IS also the Spirit of healing.

Is there an Appointed Time for My Healing?

In answering this question, let's ask another:
Is there an appointed time for salvation?

2 Corinthians 6:1-2:

"As God's co-workers we urge you not to receive God's grace in vain.
For he says, In the time of my favor I heard you, and in the day of salvation I helped you.
I tell you, now is the time of God's favor, **now** is the day of salvation. (NIV)

Rom 10:13:

For whosoever shall call upon the name of the Lord shall be saved.

Salvation is readily available since the death, burial and resurrection of our Lord Jesus Christ. Anyone, anytime, anywhere, can call upon the Lord and be saved.

Since healing was provided by the same Redemptive work, why is there a time table put on the receiving of it?

God lives in the continual NOW.
Salvation is available in the continual NOW.
Healing is also available in the continual NOW.

Usually we humans set the time for our healing......we're the ones who live in the time dimension, not God.

The woman with the issue of blood said: "If I can but touch the hem of His garment I shall be made whole."

Could she have been made whole prior to that in her own home?

She set the time for her healing by saying, 'If I can but touch the hem of his garment I shall be healed'.

This is not to criticize her, she was a very courageous woman leaving her house. Women in her condition were to be stoned if caught in public.

Because of the reports she had heard of Jesus, that the sick were brought to Him for healing, that is what she believed she had to do: get to Jesus. Her words reflect that conviction.

Since the New Covenant has NOW gone into effect, being ratified by the Blood of Jesus, what was done before the Cross in one place can be done everywhere at anytime.

This is the dispensation of the 'whosoever'!
As in, "whosoever shall call upon the Name of the Lord shall be saved".

Now faith is....
Now salvation is.....
Now healing is.....
Now peace of mind is......
Now.

The Place of the Believer's Faith in Receiving Healing

Jesus healed many people who had no faith.
Paul saw actual heathens healed, for example Acts 28:8:
"And it came to pass that the father of Publius was sick of a fever and a bloody flux: to whom Paul entered in, and prayed, and laid his hands on him and healed him."

Paul was on his way to testify at Rome. The ship he was on was destroyed in a storm, and they had washed up on the island of Melita. He calls the people there, 'barbarous'. People who knew nothing of God. That did not stop Paul in ministering healing to this man. The man was healed through the faith that Paul exercised toward God FOR him.

When **you** are a believer, however, faith is required of **you** to be healed. You can be healed on the faith of others, but the best way is to be able to receive healing on your own faith. If **you** get it, **you** can also keep it.

Mark 11:24: "what things so ever you desire, when **you** pray believe that **you** receive them and **you** shall have them (or they will manifest)."

Once you get it settled in your heart and mind that healing WAS included in Redemption, your next step is to keep yourself in a 'receiving mode'.

Really, you don't have to even 'pray', or make request for what is yours through the New Covenant. The above verse is pointing to a specific time when you 'turned the switch of faith on' and **begin** receiving.

We don't have to make request for what was given in the Redemptive Work.....we just receive, as we did with salvation. In salvation, we acknowledged what Jesus HAD DONE for us and RECEIVED IT. Healing is receiving what God HAS provided through the Redemptive Work of the Cross.

When do you believe you receive?
When you pray or turn the switch of faith on.

That is the 'set time' when *you determined* to *begin receiving* the power of God to change your situation. You don't wait to believe when you 'see' manifested what you are believing for. Your decision to receive, by faith, is the time God releases His power to bring the answer.

Remember Daniel. The answer was sent the first day he prayed, Daniel 10:12:
"Then he (the angel) said unto me (Daniel): from the first day that you set your heart to understand, and to chasten yourself before God, your words were heard and I am come with the answer to your request."

In this particular situation, it took the answer to Daniel's prayer, (he was wanting to know what would happen to his people in the future), three weeks to manifest. Note however, that the answer was SENT THE DAY HE PRAYED.

God is not holding up your answer, there are forces that hinder your receiving just as they hindered the answer to Daniel's prayer.

Physical healing begins by the power of God flowing to and then through your recreated spirit into your body. Faith, the switch of faith in the 'on' position is what get the power flowing and keeps it flowing.

It isn't God's choice to give, but your decision to receive that sets the time for receiving His healing power. At the Cross, God made available Once for All what He wanted to do for All.

Remember this Foundational Verse:
"....by His stripes you were healed", (1 Peter 2:24).

Jesus said: "Blessed are those who haven't seen and yet believe," (John 20:29).

You don't have to see immediate change in your body to believe that healing IS flowing into you, believe that you start receiving the moment you make the choice to receive.

SEE the Word of God and what it declares is yours.
SEE God watching over His Word to perform it.

At a point in time, when you appropriate healing from Isaiah or 1 Peter, see God releasing His healing power into you in response to His Word/Covenant. As you keep the switch of faith turned on, He keeps sending the healing power to you to effect a cure in your body.

METHODS OF HEALING

There are several methods of healing:

- Taking the Scriptures like you would medicine
  - Speaking the word
  - Laying on of hands
  - Anointing with oil
  - Communion

Healing by Taking the Word as Medicine

Very simply, to be healed by taking the Scriptures like medicine:

1. Don't try…..trust.
2. Put the seed in the ground.
3. The Seed is the Written Word of God.
4. The ground is your inner man.
5. Keep the Seed there.
6. Let it do its work.

See Mark 4:24-28, the Parable of the Sower.

Healing by the Word can and does take place by the Seed of God's Word sown and received in the heart. It does not require special prayers or a special anointing. God's Life in the Word produces healing. The Word is a living thing:

Heb 4:12
…for the word of God is quick, and powerful. (KJV)
…for the word of God is living, and active. (ASV)
…for whatever God says to us is full of living power. (TLB)

To receive healing through the Word, understand that there is Divine Life in the Word. That Divine Life is what brings healing and health to your body.

To receive healing by taking the Scriptures as medicine:

Come to God in faith, believing He will reward you as you seek Him, (Heb. 11:6).

Or if you are in a position like the man who said: "Lord, I believe, help my unbelief": Be in a neutral position in your soul, your mind, will and emotions. Don't have a "well I'll see if there is anything to this", kind of attitude. As I heard someone say: "If you can't believe WITH me, at least don't believe AGAINST me."

Healing may not show up in the body completely immediately after you 'take your medicine' the first time. If it does not, that isn't a sign that healing power has not been put into you by the Holy Spirit. Healing power is put into you when you put the Written Word into you. Just as salvation is imparted as you believe Scriptures concerning salvation, healing is imparted by believing Scriptures concerning healing.

Question: does the first dose of natural medicine immediately cure all your symptoms?

No, and God's Word taken as medicine works the same way.

Healing, as salvation begins in your spirit. The healing Life of God pours into your spirit through reading the Written Word. Then, that Word spoken, releases it out into your physical body.

Proverbs 4:20-22 says, "My son, attend to my words; incline your ear unto my sayings. Let them not depart from your eyes; keep them in the midst of your heart. For they are life to those that find them, and health to all their flesh."

The Hebrew words for 'health' in verse 22 is 'medicine.' God's Word is medicine to all our flesh.

Many make the mistake of substituting _belief in healing_ for the actual _taking_ of God's medicine…..His Word. They say, "I believe in healing", without actually taking the medicine. What good would it do you to believe in food if you didn't eat it? You would starve.

God's Word is His medicine.

There are several parallels between God's medicine and natural medicine.

First,
God's Word is a healing agent. His Medicine contains the capacity to produce healing. God's Word contains _inherent within it:_

> the capacity,
> the energy,
> the ability,
> the nature,

to effect healing in your body.

Stop and look at each one of those words again, and think about the fullness of what they mean.

Psalm 107:20 says, "He sent his word and healed them and delivered them from their destructions." Fenton says, "He sent out His word, and it healed and from their corruptions it freed".

Isaiah 55:10,11 says the Word of God will accomplish what it was sent out to do. Healing Scriptures contain within them the capacity to produce healing.

The key to partaking of the life and healing energy in the Word is feeding on it so that your spirit (heart) gets filled with life and energy.

Healing begins from the **inside out**…..first your inner man (spirit) is filled with the life and energy that heals, **then** through your words and actions it flows into your body. It has been my experience, that as I keep my spirit strong through the Word, I walk in an atmosphere of Divine Health.

If your symptoms are internal where they cannot be seen, reinforce your faith with Jesus' story of the fig tree. When He cursed it, the results were not immediately seen. It began to dry up 'from the roots', (Mark 11:12-24).

The Lord said to me several months ago, "sickness and disease has ears". It hears the Word when you speak it and the Word works to destroy sickness and bring health. The Word is at work IN you. Understand that healing begins, as with the fig tree's roots, in the unseen.

That is where faith comes in. Jesus said, "if you say and doubt not, you shall have what you say," (Mk 11:23). The thing you are to say is God's Word…..not your own word. God's Word has power: power to remove **and** power to restore.

Going back to Proverbs 4:20-22, "let them (My words) not depart from your eyes, keep them in the midst of your heart."

How exactly does a person do that?

First, go to the Bible and get the healing verses (or whatever you are in need of).

Next, write them down on a card (a small index card, etc), or cards. Then, put the cards up around your house so that your eyes see them several times a day. Put a card in your pocket to take with you to work or wherever you go. Put one up in the car. Get your card out, or look at it to quickly bring it to your mind and heart again.

This was a method I used before cell phones, touch pads, etc. I still would recommend it. There is something about knowing that you have taken the time to write out a particular verse(s) on a piece of paper or a card and that you can actually reach your hand into your pocket and touch it, by itself alone. Not touching a cell phone with all the other information you have in it, but a card or paper with ONLY the verse on it. Think this through, please.

Then quote it to yourself. Put your name in it: "He sent His Word and healed me." "He sends His Word and heals me."

Talk to yourself and your body about it.

When I am dealing with symptoms, I do this even more. I will wake up in the night and think on the Word…..the scriptures that I have gotten together that cover my need. I think about them when I first wake up in the morning. I say them when the symptoms act up. I go over them on my lunch hour, on my coffee breaks. I think about the Word, I speak it to myself, I thank the Father that what it says is mine, that it is at work in me right now, that He watches over His Word to perform it.

"Keep them in the midst of your heart (in your inner man), let them not depart from your eyes (or ears)" by looking at them, thinking about them, speaking them.

This is taking your medicine!

Here is a scripture for you to begin with:

Exodus 15:26: "I am the Lord that healeth thee".

This is the same verse from other translations:
….I the Lord am thy physician. (New English Bible)
….I am the Lord your life-giver. (Basic English)
….I am Yahweh thy physician. (Rotherham)
….I, Jehovah, am healing thee. (Young)
….for I, the Lord, make you immune to them (diseases).
          (Smith-Goodspeed)
….I, the Lord, will bring thee only health. (Knox)

Now, we put these different verses together, along with some others, into an affirmation or declaration of our faith:

God is speaking to me now, saying, "I am the Lord that healeth thee." He is watching over this Word to perform it. He is the Lord that heals **me**. He is healing me **now**. His Word **contains** the **ability** to **produce** what it says. His Word is **full** of healing power. I **receive** this Word **now**. I receive the healing that is **in** His Word now. Healing is inherent in God's nature. God is in me. My body is the temple of the Lord that heals me. God is bigger than sickness and Satan. God is dwelling inside of me now, healing me now. The Lord that heals me is my Shepherd; I do not lack healing. My body is in contact with the Lord that heals me. Body, respond to God's healing life and nature at work in me now. Be healed! Be whole! I command every organ and tissue of my body to be in wellness in Jesus' Name!"

Watching Your Tenses!

Another very important thing is watching your tenses. So many times we slip into the mode of still trying to 'get' healing. The Scriptures declare that healing is a finished fact, just as salvation is a finished fact. These things were finished and all made available at the Cross.

As we covered in the section on the time of your healing, in the mind of God you were saved, delivered and healed 2,000 years ago. It is just a matter of staying in the 'receiving' mode.

Any time I catch myself 'asking' for healing, I have to stop and say, "Now wait a minute.....I don't have to ask for healing. God healed me at the Cross. So I am the healed. Thank you Father, that healing is flowing to me now. It is flowing in my body now. I receive healing and health in every organ and tissue of my body. I have divine health that flows from the throne of God."

Our Foundational Scripture again:
1 Peter 2:24: "who his own self bare our sins in his body on the tree, that we being dead to sin should live unto righteousness, by whose stripes you (I) WERE (WAS) healed."

"I am working from the position of victory, of healing, of salvation, of peace. I don't have to ask God for it. He has already given it. I receive it NOW. I receive what is mine. I receive the Life, the healing that drives out sickness and disease. That healing power is mine. I believe that it is working in me right **now**."

IN TAKING YOUR MEDICINE,
WATCH YOUR TENSES!
IF YOU'RE NOT IN THE NOW,
YOU'RE NOT IN GOD'S TENSE, FOR HE IS:
"I AM"!

Healing by Speaking the Word

We see Jesus using this method.

Matthew 8:7 & 8:
"And Jesus saith unto him, I will come and heal him. The centurion answered and said, Lord, I am not worthy that you should come under my roof: but speak the word only and my servant shall be healed."

Matthew 9:6:
"Arise, take up thy bed and go unto thine house."

Matthew 9:29 & 30:
"According to your faith be it unto you. And their eyes were opened."

Examples from Acts:

Peter
Acts 3
"in the Name of Jesus Christ of Nazareth rise up and walk."
Acts 9
"Tabitha, arise."

Paul
Acts 14:8-10
And there sat a certain man at Lystra, impotent in his feet, being a cripple from his mother's womb, who never had

walked. The same heard Paul speak: who steadfastly beholding him, and perceiving that he had faith to be healed, said with a loud voice: "Stand upright on thy feet!" and he leaped and walked.

It is very important when receiving or ministering healing by speaking the Word that you make STATEMENTS not requests.

It is so with yourself and others.

You will notice that under the section, "Take Your Medicine", we concluded with an affirmation and a DECLARATION of faith.

We **affirmed** we believed God to be our healer.
Then we made a statement: "body be healed"!

These are two important parts to being healed by speaking the Word.

****

The following is an article written by Carrie Judd Montgomery, a faith pioneer of the 1800's. You will see that the importance of words is not just a creation of man during the last 50 years.

Carrie Judd Montgomery was born in Buffalo, New York, in 1858. She became an invalid at an early age and was healed through the ministry of a holiness preacher, Elizabeth Mix. Carrie's healing provided opportunities to share her testimony, and thus began her ministry that later broadened into preaching, teaching, writing, and social outreach. She moved to Oakland, California, in 1880, where she married George Montgomery, a wealthy Christian businessman. After her Pentecostal baptism in 1908, she made a worldwide tour observing the Pentecostal outpouring. Upon her return, she began publishing articles that reported the move of the Spirit around the world. Though she is probably best known for her publication, Triumphs of Faith, a journal on healing and holiness, she along with her husband established an orphanage, a missionary training school, and the Home of Peace, a haven for missionaries on furlough and other travelers.

DIVINE HEALING IN RELATION TO THE USE OF OUR LIPS
By   Carrie Judd Montgomery

Do you want to have a tongue that brings health
to yourself and to everybody around you?

An essential part of the doctrine of diving healing has to do with its relation to the right use of the lips. We find so many Christians who get out of the place of blessing through the wrong use of their tongues; so the Lord is obliged to deal with them and allow them to be sick because they have not used their tongues to His glory. We will look at some texts on this subject.

First turn to Psalm 139:4: "For there is not a word in my tongue, but, lo, O Lord, thou knowest it altogether." If the Lord Jesus were personally visible to us, we would be very careful about our conversation. If, when we went out, we could see Him visibly walking by our side, how careful we would be about our words; but because we do not fully realize His presence with us, we often are not as careful as we should be. We speak the little hasty word, the impetuous word, the word that is not just as kind and tender as it ought to be, and the Holy Spirit is so faithful that He will reprove us. Sometimes we are not loving and tender in our speech because we misunderstand others. The Lord wants us to be meek, and leaning upon Him every moment so that He will not let us judge after the sight of our eyes or the hearing of our ears. I often pray this prayer, "O God, do not let me judge after the sight of my eyes, but let me know about everything as the Holy Spirit reveals it to me." "He shall teach you all things." This means that He will teach us moment by moment, and we are not to judge things by our own understanding. How solemn to realize that Jesus is listening to our every word! Beloved, I am sure that we all want to please Him in every word and every thought-and yet we are so slow to comprehend that complete yieldedness to Him that will enable Him to work in us to will and to do of His good pleasure.

Now we will look at Proverbs 18:21. Here we read these remarkable words: "Death and life are in the power of the tongue." We take this in two different ways. There are many cases where an infuriated man will speak angry words that stir up anger in another person, which may lead to murder or some desperate act, and in that sense life and death are in the power of the tongue to the sinner; but there is another sense in which life and death are in the power of the tongue to God's children. If we disobey Him and speak words that divide God's children, or if we speak words that grieve God's little ones and wound them to the heart, God is greatly displeased. I believe that if sick people would let God search them, He would often show them that long years ago there was a time when they wounded God's little ones, or when they caused separation among some of God's children, so that God's heart was greatly grieved; and He would show them that they are suffering for it today. Repentance and confession and trust in the cleansing blood will bring them to the place of blessing and healing. Oh, I do believe, dear friends, that we are not filled enough with the Word of God. The psalmist said, "Thy word have I hid in mine heart, that I might not sin against thee." If we are filled with His Word we shall walk softly, and our tongues will be controlled by the Lord.

Proverbs 12:18. Here are two different kinds of speech: "There is that speaketh like the piercings of a sword: but the tongue of the wise is health." How sad it seems to think that any of God's children could speak like the piercings of a sword, but if the tongue is not sanctified it will sometimes speak in that sharp way
and pierce the hearts of some of God's children. Of such a person God might say, "But whoso shall offend one of these little ones which believe in me, it were better for him that a millstone were hanged about his neck, and that he were drowned in the depth of the sea." I do not know whether this appeals to you as solemnly as it ought, but God has made it mean so much-and by our words we shall be justified or condemned.

Then we read of the other kind of a tongue-the tongue of the wise that is health. Do you want to have a tongue that brings health to yourself and to everybody around you-through which Jesus can speak His words of love and life? Even if God shows you that another soul needs to be dealt with about some sin, let us be so tender with them that we can say in the words of the Master, "Neither do I condemn thee." When we deal with people who have done wrong, they know in a moment if we are critical and harsh, or if we are seeking to help them into a place of blessing.

Proverbs 15:4. "A wholesome tongue is a tree of life: but perverseness therein is a breach in the spirit." "A wholesome tongue is a tree of life" in your own being and also in the one to whom you are speaking. You say, "I would like to have a tree of life in me." Christ is the tree of life, and when we have Christ fully formed in us we have His life for soul and body.

"Out of the abundance of the heart the mouth speaketh," so if you are quite full of divine love, you will never say anything but loving words. Then people who are hungry-hearted will feel Christ's love in you, and even those who are in erroneous doctrines, but are not satisfied, will feel this love and will desire to be taught the way of life.

Turn to Proverbs 13:3. "He that keepeth his mouth keepeth his life." If we keep our mouth from all evil speaking and from all guile, our physical life as well as our spiritual life will be kept by the Lord. When you are sick and cannot get healed, wait on God and let Him search you. Do not try to search out things yourself, but let the light of heaven stream in. As the Lord shows you your failure to keep your lips under the blood, repent and confess to Him and to those whom you have injured.

Now, let us read Psalm 15:3. This is a wonderful psalm. It opens in this way: "Lord, who shall abide in thy tabernacle? who shall dwell in thy holy hill?" Then follows a description of the kind of person who abides in His taber-nacle-in the secret place of the Most High; and you know that if we abide in Christ we may ask what we will and it shall be done unto us. The second verse reads: "He that walketh uprightly, and worketh righteousness, and speaketh the truth in his heart." And the third, "He that backbiteth not with his tongue, nor doeth evil to his neighbour, nor taketh up a reproach against his neighbour." We are to dwell continually in that secret place of His holy hill where we do not backbite with our tongues and we do not take up a reproach against another. Those who take up a reproach tell it to somebody else-until it is cast abroad like the seeds of a poisonous weed. This is indeed evil in the sight of the Lord.

I heard of one lady who, when anybody brought her an evil report, would say, "Come, let us go together to that one and see if it is true." This stopped people from coming to her with their backbiting. The Word is so plain to us that if we have anything against another, we are to go to that one alone. The devil will bring up a thousand reasons why we cannot do this, but we must obey God-and usually we will find that the trouble will fade away like the mist before the sun.

Next we will read I Peter 3:8-10: "Finally, be ye all of one mind." What kind of mind? It looks as though our minds are very different one from another, but this is the kind of mind that we are to have alike: "Having compassion one of another, love as brethren, be pitiful, be courteous: Not rendering evil for evil, or railing for railing: but contrariwise blessing; knowing that ye are thereunto called, that ye should inherit a blessing." I especially want to call our attention to this next verse: "For he that will love life, and see good days, let him refrain his tongue from evil, and his lips that they speak no guile."

The company we read of in Revelation 14, who followed the Lamb whithersoever He went, had this characteristic: "In their mouth was found no guile." That means no deceit-not changing things just a little, but letting the One who is true dwell in us and speak through us. "I am the . . . truth," Jesus said; and the Holy Spirit is called the Spirit of truth. As we are filled with the Spirit He will make us true and cause us to speak the exact truth.

"He that will love life, and see good days . . ." We love life because Christ is our life-even here and now. We love life because we can serve Him-because we can bring many sheaves and lay them down at our Master's feet. "Good days." Our days are not good days if they are full of sickness. If we keep our tongues from evil and if we speak no guile, we may claim from the Lord good days-full of His joy, and full of His life and health.

Turn to James 1:26: "If any man among you seem to be religious, and bridleth not his tongue, but deceiveth his own heart, this man's religion is vain." This is one of the most solemn verses that we have read. A person may "seem" to be very religious but use his tongue in a wrong way, and God says, "This man's religion is vain." Such a man is deceived, and has no real heart-religion.

James 3:5-8: "Even so the tongue is a little member, and boasteth great things. Behold, how great a matter a little fire kindleth! And the tongue is a fire, a world of iniquity: so is the tongue among our members, that it defileth the whole body, and setteth on fire the course of nature; and it is set on fire of hell." This is a description of the untamed tongue that belongs to a person who has not been saved. Read the rest of the passage: "For every kind of beasts, and of birds, and of serpents, and of things in the sea, is tamed, and hath been tamed of mankind: But the tongue can no man tame; it is an unruly evil, full of deadly poison." No man can tame the tongue, but God can tame it. It is subdued and tamed through being saved and filled with the Holy Ghost. How precious that God can use a sanctified and yielded tongue to give forth His wonderful messages of life.

If we have a bottle of deadly poison in the house we put a label on it, with skull and crossbones; and if those who go around speaking evil and backbiting and making division could be labeled deadly poison, people would be on their guard; unfortunately, they do not wear a label. People who do such things need not think that they will go free, for God will surely deal with them. Now notice the thirteenth verse of this same chapter: "Who is a wise man and endued with knowledge among you? let him shew out of a good conversation his works with meekness of wisdom." Our conversation shows where we stand spiritually.

Look at Psalm 101:5: "Whoso privily slandereth his neighbour, him will I cut off." I believe God sometimes cuts off from the earth those who will not yield to Him when He disciplines them for slandering others. This is very solemn. May God search His people along these lines-and have mercy upon them.

Now read Isaiah 50:4: "The Lord God hath given me the tongue of the learned, that I should know how to speak a word in season to him that is weary: he wakeneth morning by morning, he wakeneth mine ear to hear as the learned."

Oh, that we may be taught of God's Holy Spirit to speak sweet, gentle words of comfort and tenderness to him that is weary. How precious to speak a word in season, before one might come to the point of despair, and to see that one lifted up into His courage and joy.

Turn to Song of Solomon 5:13. Nobody can understand this book unless the Holy Spirit explains it. It must be a very spiritual heart and mind that approaches it, and it is full of instruction for the bride of Christ. We read in the latter part of this verse, which refers to Jesus, "His lips like lilies, dropping sweet smelling myrrh." Earlier, in 4:3, we read of the lips of His bride as being "like a thread of scarlet." The blood must be over her lips, but His lips are like lilies; and when our lips are covered with the scarlet blood they will bring forth the lilies of His own purity.

We will now turn to the sixth chapter of Isaiah. Isaiah saw the King and realized that his own lips were unclean. Minnie Abrams told us about a girl at Ramabai's in India, at the time of a great revival there, who kept crying out, "O Lord, Thou art holy, but I am vile." She had a vision of the King; and when we have that vision of the Lord in the beauty of His holiness, we see what we are in ourselves and how we need His blood to cleanse us. How were Isaiah's lips cleansed? We read that one of the seraphim took a live coal and laid it on his lips, and his sin was purged. But where did the angel get the coal? He took it from off the altar.

God's holiness would burn us to death if God did not take it from off the altar of Christ's atoning sacrifice. "And he laid it upon my mouth, and said, Lo, this hath touched thy lips; and thine iniquity is taken away, and thy sin purged." Then he was ready, when the Lord asked who would go for Him, to say, "Here am I; send me." We all need the coal of fire from off Christ's altar of sacrifice to touch our hearts and our lips.

What kind of lips does God want us to have? See Ephesians 5:18-20. God's command is to "Be filled with the Spirit." And when we are filled with the Spirit, what shall we be doing? "Speaking to yourselves in psalms and hymns and spiritual songs, singing and making melody in your heart to the Lord; Giving thanks always for all things unto God and the Father in the name of our Lord Jesus Christ." Is it not wonderful that God will bend to hear the melody in our hearts-when heaven is so full of melody? "Giving thanks always for all things." We will have a tongue full of worship, full of thanksgiving to God, praising Him for everything that He allows-even for the trials-because they are all going to work together for good to them that love God.

One more text-Matthew 21:15-16. Here we read of "the children crying in the temple, and saying, Hosanna to the Son of David." And we read that the chief priests and scribes "were sore displeased, And said unto him, Hearest thou what these say?" How those untrue men hated the praise of the little children. Jesus said, "Yea; have ye never read, Out of the mouth of babes and sucklings thou hast perfected praise?" The Lord was quoting from the eighth Psalm, and we will read it from the Old Testament. The wording here is wonderful: "Out of the mouth of babes and sucklings hast thou ordained strength because of thine enemies, that thou mightest still the enemy and the avenger." So we can put the two things together-praise and strength; that is, if we will praise God it will make us strong. God ordains strength through the perfection of praise, and this praise stills the enemy and the avenger.

I believe we have not fully understood how much praise means in the winning of a battle. We must get to the place where we pray through-and get on to praising ground. Then we shall be like children in the perfection of our praise. Jesus said,

"Except ye be converted, and become as little children, ye shall not enter into the kingdom of heaven." Little children never criticize each other; they never doubt your word: Their guilelessness is wonderful. The reason we criticize each other is that we doubt one another's motives. There is one special verse that ought to stop our doing that: "For thou that judgest doest the same things." (Romans 2:1). That means if we impute a wrong motive to another's actions, we do it because there is the same thing in us.

Beloved, let us seek to be filled with the love that is described in the thirteenth chapter of I Corinthians-and when our hearts are filled with this love our lips will be also.

****

(I have just recently heard of studies that medical science has been conducting about the relationship of words to physical healing. Their conclusions are confirming the truths of Scripture set forth above. AW, 1/14)

Healing Through Laying On Of Hands

Jesus' example:

Matthew 8:3
"And Jesus put forth his hand, and touched him saying, I will, be thou clean. And immediately his leprosy was cleansed."

Matthew 8:14
"And when Jesus was come into Peter's house, he saw his wife's mother laid, and sick of a fever, and he touched her hand and the fever left her: and she arose and ministered unto them."

Paul's example:
Acts 19:11
"and God wrought special miracles by the hands of Paul: so that from his body were brought unto the sick handkerchiefs or aprons, and the diseases departed from them and the evil spirits went out of them."

Acts 28:8 & 9
"And it came to pass that the father of Publius lay sick of a fever and of a bloody flux: to whom Paul entered in and prayed, and laid his hands on him, and healed him. So when this was done others also which had diseases in the island came and were healed."

Why the laying on of hands?
It is one of the ways that God ministers His healing power to people. He transmits His power through the hands of the believer that come into contact with the body of the person who is sick.

When hands are laid on you, we are operating in obedience to the law of contact and transmission. As we do God flows into your body through the faith of those ministering to you…..His power, life, virtue, anointing.

You receive whether you feel anything or not.

The tangibility of the Holy Spirit is *sensed and received* by your spirit, not usually felt your body.

The tangibility of the Holy Spirit, (the anointing that heals), then flows from your spirit into your body, just as it flows out of the spirit and through the hands of those who are ministering to you.

No matter what your condition, this tangible Holy Spirit can break anything off, fix or repair anything, create anything.

You may see an immediate physical change.

Even if you do not, believe that you have received and that the Presence of God has come in to effect healing in your body.   Remember the fig tree, and the lepers who were healed *as they went*.

Position your will when you have hands laid on you. Be sure that those doing the praying believe it **is** God's will to heal today and know how to pray **the prayer of faith**.

After prayer, do not be moved off of the fact that the healing power of God **was** imparted to you and is at work in you.

Go your way rejoicing.

Receive further ministry as needed for complete wellness.

Determine to begin living a life of wellness, by embarking on a mission, a mission to learn all you can about the Redemption provided for your healing.

And then living by what you have learned.
A life of wellness is possible....for the rest of your life.

Healing is getting well.
Wellness is the state of living in continuous healing.

Die without sickness and disease, as the Old Testament saints.

Even on the Cross, in all the redemptive agony that Jesus was suffering, He chose the moment of His death: 'Father, into thy hands I commend my spirit'.

The same Jesus, in you, can release your spirit to the Father without sickness.

We are convinced that God will do the work in your body.
Your part is to receive.

Healing by Anointing with Oil & The Prayer of Faith

There is only one verse in the New Testament related to the practice of anointing with oil the sick when you are ministering healing to them. It is in James 5:14 & 15:

"Is any sick among you? Let him call for the elders of the church; and let them pray over him, anointing him with oil in the name of the Lord, and the prayer of faith shall save the sick and the Lord shall raise him up; and if he have committed sins, they shall be forgiven him. Confess your faults one to another and pray one for another that you may be healed. The effectual fervent prayer of a righteous man availeth much."

We do not see Jesus anointing with oil, neither is there a record of it being done in the book of Acts. This practice was developed as the Church grew. You will notice from this verse, that healing can precede the forgiveness of sins.

Also, it is the 'prayer of faith' that saves the sick……there are no supernatural properties in the oil.

Healing Illustrated in Communion

1 Corinthians 11:23-33:

"For I have received of the Lord that which also I delivered unto you, that the Lord Jesus the same night in which he was betrayed took bread: And when he had given thanks, he brake it, and said, Take, eat: this is my body, which is broken for you: this do in remembrance of me. After the same manner also he took the cup, saying, this cup is the new testament in my blood: this do, as often as you drink it, in remembrance of me. For as often as you eat this bread, and drink this cup, you do show the Lord's death till he come. Wherefore whosoever shall eat this bread, and drink this cup of the Lord, unworthily, shall be guilty of the body and blood of the Lord. But let a man examine himself, and so let him eat of that bread, and drink of that cup. For he that eats and drinks unworthily, eats and drinks damnation to himself, not discerning the Lord's body. For this cause many are weak and sickly among you, and many sleep. For if we would judge ourselves, we should not be judged.

But when we are judged, we are chastened of the Lord, that we should not be condemned with the world."

We know there are two elements used in communion: the bread representing the broken body of the Lord Jesus and the cup representing His Blood shed for the forgiveness of our sins.

Since the cup represents forgiveness, what does the bread represent?

Healing for the body.

The verses regarding 'eating and drinking unworthily' are usually interpreted to mean taking communion with sin in the heart and for that reason the judgment of God comes upon people and they die an early death through some type of calamity or sickness. That certainly can apply.

Thinking 'outside the box' of traditional interpretation, however:

Could they be sick and dying early because when they are taking of the bread they are not understanding that it represents the body of Jesus broken for their healing: "by his stripes you were healed"?

Could this be the meaning of "not discerning the Lord's body?"

Not discerning, or rightly understanding, that the Lord's body bore the stripes of the scourging for the healing of our bodies?

If the bread doesn't represent healing for the body, why take it?

We could just take the Cup, representing the Blood of Jesus shed for the remission of our sins.

When we judge ourselves as to what we are believing about the body of Jesus bearing the stripes for our healing, what we believe about that will either save us or condemn us with the world.

The world dies early because they do not discern that Jesus bore stripes for their healing.

Of course, this is all the working of faith……..
Just as faith in the Blood for forgiveness is released when we take the cup, faith in the Body for healing is to be released when we take the bread.

How is it exactly that healing takes place?

- The Holy Spirit is tangible...

Mark 5:30
"Jesus said, who touched me for I perceive that virtue has gone out of me."

This is a remarkable section of scripture. It makes clear in no uncertain terms that the Spirit of God has substance.....spiritual substance. The Holy Spirit was in Jesus, the Holy Spirit flowed out of Him and into the woman, resulting in instant healing in her body.

Jesus actually sensed or perceived that the Holy Spirit had flowed out of Him. He would not have been able to do that if the Holy Spirit had no tangibility.

Jesus 'sensed or perceived' that out flowing. Because Jesus was aware that He was a spirit and that God the Spirit was in Him, Jesus was sensitive to those inward movings and flowings of the Spirit.

Most of the time we are trained to be physically, emotionally or mentally sensitive, but we are not trained to sense the movings and flowings of the Spirit.

Psychics and such people are aware of the demonic spirit-world movings.

Christians also must be aware of the Holy Spirit movings.

THE TANGIBILITY OF THE SPIRIT
By John G. Lake

It is one of the most difficult things in all the world for people who are not familiar with the ministry of healing to comprehend that the Spirit of God is a tangible, actual, living quantity, just as real as electricity, just as real as any other native force. Yea and a great deal more so. (It is) The life principle that stands behind all manifestations of life everywhere.

Men, by the action of the will, take themselves out of the control of the power of the law of sin and death, and by the action of their will place themselves **consciously in union and in touch** with the law of the Spirit of Life.

The Holy Spirit flows into you when you do this and brings healing to you just as he brought healing to the woman with the issue of blood.

****

- You use the same faith for healing as you did for salvation.

Your faith receives for you.......

1) forgiveness for sin
Luke 7:36-50:
This is the story of the Pharisee who invited Jesus to come to his home and eat. While there, the woman came in who brought an alabaster box if ointment. She anointed his feet, and washed his feet with her tears, wiping them dry with her hair. In this context, the 'saved' being spoken of is from sin, for Vs. 50 says in particular, "thy faith hath saved (Gk **sozo**) thee, go in peace."

2) healing for body
Luke 8:48: And He said unto her, "Daughter be of good comfort, your faith has made you whole (saved, GK **sozo**). Go in peace and be whole (sozo) of your plague."

In this context, the 'saved' being spoken of is from sickness. The issue of blood she had for twelve years dried up.

The same Greek word: 'sozo' is used in both cases and translated for us as the English word, 'saved' and 'whole'.

The very same faith that saves the soul also will heal the body.

What does '**sozo**' mean: to save one suffering from disease, to heal to make whole; to preserve from danger, to rescue; to deliver from the penalties of Judgment. (Strong's #4983)

Post-Prayer Instructions

If you have someone lay hands on you for healing, lay hands on yourself or pray the prayer of faith according to Mark 11:24, please do the following afterwards:

1. Do not speak any words that do not agree with the Scriptures and/or the prayer of faith.

2. Do not base the reality of whether the healing anointing was imparted to you on whether or not you "felt" anything. (Since man looks on the outward but God looks on the inward, we must leave it totally up to God as to whether or not we "feel" anything when ministered to.) Remember; The less faith you have, the more God must give you "feelings" to help collaborate what He is doing in your spirit and body. By the same token, the more faith you have, the less you will need to "feel something"

3. There is no limit to the number of times you may be ministered to for healing. No problem is too large or too small. You are NOT praying the same prayer over and over. You are receiving the ministry of the Spirit.

4. You should read Healing Scriptures at least 3 times per day. Each time, they should be read out loud with force. Reading them more often will only help and cannot hurt. You cannot overdose.

5. When your healing manifests, you must tell others what has occurred. Give glory to God for healing you.

6. If at all possible you should pray for someone else that has a need. The best way to pray for someone is to pray with the same force and attitude with which you were prayed for.

ROMANS 8:2
THE NEW LAW OF YOUR LIFE

To conclude our section on healing, let's look at this verse:

Rom 8:2
For the law of the Spirit of life in Christ Jesus hath made me free from the law of sin and death.   KJV

….. For the power of the life-giving Spirit-and this power is mine through Christ Jesus-has freed me from the vicious circle of sin and death. The Living Bible

Summed up in this one verse is the 'ax laid to the root of the tree' of sickness and disease.

The law of sin and death, (this is not the Law of God which is good), is the law that rules this world since Adam. This law produces sin and death in all its forms.

For those in Christ, they are under a new law: the Law of the Spirit of Life. This Law sets you free from the law Adam loosed. The Holy Spirit, Who is the Spirit of Life, will keep you now, preserve you now, and in the life to come give your body immortality.

Read the following commentary in that light:

Rom 8:2: Jamieson, Faucett & Brown commentary (the picture of the new reality IN you that this commentary presents is very powerful. Read slowly and picture in your mind what is being said. The 'strong man armed' is the sinful nature along with its law of sin and death. The 'stronger than he' is Jesus and the Law of the Spirit of Life.)

Let us now observe the import of this pregnant phrase, "the Spirit of life in Christ Jesus." He is called "the Spirit of life," as opening up in the souls of believers a fountain of spiritual life (see John 7:38-39). And as the word "law" here has, beyond all reasonable doubt, the same meaning as in Rom 7:23 - namely, 'an inward principle of action, operating with the fixedness and regularity of a law,' it thus appears that "the law of the Spirit of life in Christ Jesus" here means, 'that new principle of action which the Spirit of Christ has opened up within us-the law of our new being.

This "sets us free," as soon as it takes possession of our inner man, "from the law of sin and death," - i.e., from the enslaving power of that corrupt principle which carries death in its bosom. The "strong man armed" is overpowered by the "Stronger than he;" the weaker principle is dethroned and expelled by the more powerful; the principle of spiritual life prevails against and brings into captivity the principle of spiritual death - "leading captivity captive." If this now be the apostle's meaning, the "For," with which the verse opens, does not assign the reason, but supplies the evidence of what goes before (as in Luke 7:47, and other places); in other words, the meaning is not, 'There is no condemnation to believers, because they have gotten the better of their inward corruption' (very different doctrine this certainly from the apostle's); but 'The triumph of believers over their inward corruption, through the power of Christ's Spirit in them, proves them to be in Christ Jesus, and as such absolved from condemnation.'

Developing your ability to WALK IN the reality that Romans 8:2 tells you that you are living in, is the surest way to enjoy divine health.

Divine healing is an individual operation of the Law of the Spirit of Life..... Divine health is the continuous operation of the Law of the Spirit of Life in Christ Jesus. Just as we grow in all other areas of our Christian life, we should also grow in our ability to walk in the Life that is in Christ Jesus Who is IN us.

Removing Roadblocks to Healing

Roadblock #1:   Your understanding of the sovereignty of God.

I would like to include here for your study and thought the following article.......it will definitely challenge your current understanding of the sovereignty of God and hopefully broaden your horizons.   Your understanding of the sovereignty of God is either a channel or a roadblock to receiving physical healing.

WHAT IS THE SOVEREIGNTY OF GOD?

by
Pastor Steven T. Hall
Rivers of Living Water Church
pastorsteve7@bellsouth.net

I believe one of the most destructive doctrines in the Church today is how the **"Sovereignty of God"** is taught. It is one of the greatest deceptions the devil has birthed in the Church. It literally makes our efforts and actions irrelevant.

The word **"sovereign"** is not used in the King James Version of the Bible. It is used 303 times in the Old Testament of the New International Version, but it is always used in association with the word "LORD" and is the equivalent of the King James Version's "Lord God." Not a single one of those times is the word **"sovereign"** used in the manner that it has come to be used in religion in our day and time. Where does our doctrine of the **"Sovereignty of God"** originate?

One of the most influential of the early Church fathers, Augustine, was very instrumental in the development and propagation of many of the church doctrines we hold so tightly to today including, **"The Sovereignty of God."**

He theorized and developed a theological teaching that there is no such thing as evil. He said, "it wasn't evil; it was just how you perceive it to be." "If you really knew the intent of God, everything that looks like it is bad in your life, is not bad." "God allows this to happen;" "He doesn't cause it, but He allows it to happen for the good in your life."
These concepts have been taught to literally hundreds of thousands of pastors, teachers, and layman alike. Through these students, the error has multiplied, literally paralyzing millions within the Church.

"Hosea 4:6 My people are destroyed for lack of knowledge. Because you have rejected knowledge, I also will reject you from being priest for Me; Because you have forgotten the law of your God, I also will forget your children.

The great error in Augustine's theology, is with everyone believing that it is part of God's will for us to experience sickness, disease, and poverty. It kills the believer's faith and makes the body of believer's powerless against these things.   If Augustine's theology is correct, and it is God's will for you to have sickness, disease, and poverty, then for you to pray against these things would be useless since you would be praying against God's will for your life or your loved ones.

Augustine's teaching infers that God is using some tragedy or disease to teach you some deep spiritual truth and all suffering is for some greater good.

It is true that we can learn from tragedies and hardships, but God has not orchestrated the tragedies or hardships in our lives to teach us.

Yes, it is true that God continually teaches us but His way of teaching is not to destroy our lives: _"He has come that we may have life and have it abundantly" (Jn. 10:10b)._ God gave to you and I His Word, the Holy Spirit, and the Anointing that lives in us as our teachers.

If you deny that evil exists, you are denying that Satan and the hordes of demons under his control exist. By accepting Augustine's theology you are ACCEPTING ANYTHING the devil decides to put upon you as if it were from God. Can't you see the danger in that? Do you realize that many of the doctrines the majority of the modern Church holds to and teaches today are doctrines written by men who CANNOT AND NEVER HAVE WALKED IN THE POWER OF THE GOSPEL OF JESUS CHRIST? These men, because of their powerlessness, have developed doctrines and traditions to justify their IMPOTENCE. The Church needs to throw off every doctrine and tradition that Jesus Christ has not given to us. If it is not in the New Covenant, then, "IT IS NOT!"

****

Another item on this subject by Andrew Womack:

Religion has resulted in the invention of a new meaning for the word **"sovereign,"** which basically means: "God controls everything". Nothing can happen but what He wills or allows. However, there is nothing in the actual definition that states that. The dictionary defines **"sovereign"** as:

1. Paramount; supreme, excellent.
2. Having supreme rank or power.
3. Independent: a sovereign state.

None of these definitions means that God controls everything. (_Andrew Womack, article_ "The Sovereignty of God.")

Roadblock #2: Healing passed away with the last apostle

Church history through the years after the early apostles died, has testimony after testimony of people being healed. Healing always accompanied a 'living faith' in the fact that Jesus is the Same, yesterday, today and forever.

The same is true today.

Roadblock #3: God chasten with sickness.

Does God send sickness to chasten us for not being in His will or for being disobedient? That cannot be proven by the example of Jesus, the early Church or the New Covenant.

How does He chastise His own? With His Word.

Second Timothy 3:16-17:
"Every Scripture is God-breathed, given by His inspiration, and is profitable for instruction, for reproof and conviction of sin, for correction of error and discipline in obedience, and for training in righteousness, so that the man of God may be complete and proficient, well fitted and thoroughly equipped for   every   good   work"   (TheAmplifiedBible).

If you'll look in 2 Corinthians 7, Paul talks about a situation in the **Corinthian church that needed correction....a man was living** in an intimate relationship with his father's wife.

How did Paul do it? Not by asking God to send an earthquake to shake them up! He did it by writing them a letter. It cut deep into their spirits and brought them to repentance.

The young man was removed from the fellowship of the church and came to repentance. Paul had also told them that if he did not repent, they were to "turn him over to Satan for the destruction of the flesh that his soul might be saved".

This 'destruction of the flesh' was not an option for a person in good standing in the church. God does not pick out a wonderful Christian person and 'turn them over to Satan for the destruction of the flesh'. Take a good look at the context. This destructive action was only to be taken as a last resort.

Let's look at some word definitions here:

Affliction and Chastening

When people quote Scripture passages to explain their having sickness by saying, "many are the afflictions of the righteous" or "God chastens His children", you realize what their understanding is about the source of their sickness. To them, God is behind their illness and troubles.

However, the words afflictions and chastenings in those passages quoted do not mean sicknesses or diseases.

Psalm 34:19 in the King James Version begins with, "Many are the afflictions of the righteous." Notice that it does not say, "Many are the sicknesses of the righteous," but even if it did say this, the verse ends with, "but the Lord ***delivers*** them out of them all."

The truth is that the word 'afflictions' in Psalm 34:19 means anguish, burdened, persecution, tribulation, trouble, (Strong's Dictionary). This word does not mean 'sicknesses'.

What about 'the chastening of the Lord'? What really is the 'chastening of the Lord'? Here is that passage in the NIV:

"The Lord disciplines ['chastens' in the KJV] those he loves, and he punishes everyone he accepts as a son. Endure hardship as discipline; God is treating you as sons. For what son is not disciplined by his father?" (Hebrews 12:6-7)

In my search of _men's translations and commentaries_, the word 'punish' was consistently used with the thought that God 'sends' trials upon the children that He loves and that the trial is of His 'sovereign' choosing and wisdom. Therefore, we should not question the 'why' of the trial, just embrace it and try to find out what God is teaching us through it.

This interpretation is based primarily on looking at the New Testament through an Old Testament mindset. God did bring Israel to repentance through physical hardship, but that was the only avenue open to Him, as their hearts were hard.

In the New Testament He has 'taken out the stony heart and put in us a heart of flesh'. He has put His Spirit in us. He has written His laws on the tables of our hearts and **speaks** correction to us in our tender hearts. That is why Jesus said over and over: "be careful how you hear." And "he that has an ear to hear, let him hear what the Spirit says to the churches."

With this interpretation of God chastening with sickness and calamity being promoted through commentaries and pulpits, it is no wonder that the picture of God as the 'source of all things, including troubles' is so prevalent. (Refer back to the section on the 'Sovereignty of God').

In truth, the word 'chasten' or 'discipline' means instruct, learn, teach, (Strong's Greek Dictionary).

What kind of parents would instruct or even discipline their beloved children by inflicting cancer or AIDS or any other disease on them? God is a God who loves His children and has our best interests at heart. He is not a God of child abuse.

Looking at this verse from the traditional viewpoint, if we DID believe that sicknesses are 'chastenings', what does the passage above instruct us to do? We are instructed _**to endure**_ chastenings!

If we believe that sicknesses are 'chastenings' then we should not go to a doctor nor take any medication nor do anything to alleviate our symptoms or to try to get better, because then we're not enduring our discipline.

Afflictions and chastenings _do not mean sicknesses_.

Paul gave us several long lists of trials that he went through, and not only endured but boasted about (2 Corinthians 6:4-10, 11:23-28, 12:7-10). There is not a single example of sickness or disease in any of those lists of afflictions.

Unfortunately, many people are misunderstanding and misusing these Scriptures and are imprisoned in their sicknesses, diseases and infirmities. Wouldn't you rather believe what the Bible really says and be healed of your sickness and pain?

Remember the three foundations we are building upon for a life of wellness: The Word, The Example of Jesus, The Cross.

Did Jesus ever put sickness on anyone to teach them a spiritual lesson?

Roadblock 4. Traditional Understanding of Paul's 'Thorn'

What was Paul's 'thorn in the flesh'?

There has been a lot of speculation about this, but Paul tells us exactly what it was....a "messenger of Satan" (2 Corinthians 12:7).

Nowhere in the New Testament does this word messenger or angel (angelos in the Greek) ever refer to sickness or disease. It always refers to sentient, living beings (usually angels, but sometimes humans).

Paul did not use a Greek word for sickness or disease in this verse. He specifically used the Greek word for 'angel', and he told us that it was a demonic angel, a messenger of Satan.

Notice in the passage above that Paul did not ask God to heal him, he asked God to take away (aphistemi) the 'thorn'. There is a big difference.

This is the same Greek word that is used in Acts 12:10 when the angel 'departed' (aphistemi), from Peter.

In all of the 15 other occurrences of this word in the Greek New Testament it is never used in reference to sickness or healing (see Luke 2:37, 4:13, 8:13, 13:27, Acts 5:37, 38,

15:38, 19:9, 22:29, 1 Timothy 4:1, 6:5, 2 Timothy 2:19, and Hebrews 3:12).

Paul wasn't asking for a sickness to be healed, he was asking God to take away this demonic harassment.

Nowhere in the New Testament is there even a single example of anyone <u>pleading with God to healing them</u>.

Jesus never pled with God to heal anyone. The apostles never did. No one ever pled with Jesus to heal them.

This is not how healing works....pleading for God to come and heal, and this is never how Paul healed anyone in the New Testament.

Paul was not pleading for a healing! He was pleading to be delivered from *persecutions and hardships*.

Demons are personalities just as people are, except that they do not have their own bodies. Paul specifically said that his 'thorn' was a demon which was bringing suffering upon him everywhere he went, which is exactly the same way that a 'thorn' in the flesh is used everywhere else in Scripture. It has nothing to do with sickness or disease.

When we read the book of Acts and all of Paul's letters, it is easy to see that it was never a part of Paul's doctrine or teachings that sickness is a 'thorn in the flesh' to be patiently endured.

God strengthened Paul to complete his ministry in spite of this demonic harassment. Paul grew in grace and understanding of how to deal with demonic spirits. This can be seen in comparing 2 Corinthians to Ephesians. Second Corinthians was written 5 years before Ephesians

Roadblock #5: Paul's 'Eye Condition'

Tying right into Paul's thorn, it is traditionally taught that Paul's thorn was an eye condition ...... chronic ophthalmia.

Notice that Paul said he had a bodily ailment (which is often taken to be this eye problem) when he first visited Galatia:

"You know that it was on account of a bodily ailment that [I remained and] preached the Gospel to you the first time. And [yet], although my physical condition was [such] a trial to you, you did not regard it with contempt, for I bear witness that you would have torn out your own eyes and given them to me [to replace mine], if that were possible." (Galatians 4:13-15, AMP)

The NIV uses the word 'illness' in this passage, but the Greek is literally 'infirmity (or weakness) of the flesh'.

What was this infirmity of the flesh or this bodily ailment? Acts 14:19-20 tells us that when Paul and Barnabas were in Lystra, the crowd stoned Paul and left him for dead. The next day, Paul and Barnabas went to Derbe, which was in the southern part of Galatia (according to Eerdman's Atlas of the Bible):

"Then some Jews came from Antioch and Iconium and won the crowd over. They stoned Paul and dragged him outside the city, thinking he was dead. But after the disciples had gathered around him, he got up and went back into the city. The **_next day_** he and Barnabas left for Derbe." (Acts 14:19-20)

Have you ever seen a person after a stoning? The main place aimed for is the head! That wouldn't be too good on the eyes either!

Paul preached and practiced healing, and not once did he ever tell anyone to patiently endure sicknesses, nor did he ever say that he himself was patiently enduring any infirmity. If Paul's eyes were wounded during the stoning, they apparently were healed because he never listed any eye problems among the sufferings he had received for the sake of the Gospel.

In fact, in Paul's very last letter he asked Timothy to bring him his scrolls and parchments (2 Timothy 4:13), which would imply that he intended to read them.

Roadblock #6: "If it be Thy will....."

Only one time in the four Gospels and the Book of Acts is this question asked, and yet tradition makes it a part of every prayer for healing.

"And there came a leper to him, beseeching him, and kneeling down to him, and saying unto him, If thou wilt, thou canst make me clean. And Jesus moved with compassion, put forth his hand, and touched him, and saith unto him, I will, be thou clean. And as soon as he had spoken, immediately the leprosy departed from him and he was cleansed."

Lepers were unclean. No one touched them. When people would come near, they had to cry, "Unclean! Unclean!"

It is logical that this leper would ask Jesus _**'if'**_ He would heal him. There had been no report of Jesus previously healing someone with leprosy. People usually came for healing because they 'heard the fame of Him'. This leper had heard of Jesus healing people, but nothing regarding Jesus healing lepers. He could have no confidence for something he didn't know was Jesus desire. In the leper's mind, it was even unlawful for Jesus to touch him.

In Jesus' answer, we find that the question of, 'if it be thy will', settled. He said, "I WILL, be thou clean!"

Why do we still ask this question when it has been settled?

Was there anyone who came to Jesus for healing that said, "if it be thy will" again?

We don't think these things through with the Mind of Christ and therefore we perish for lack of knowledge.

From Divine Healing to Divine Health (Wellness)

I would like to include here a short quote by Gordon Lindsey, Founder of Christ for the Nations in his book, "The Bible Secret of Divine Health".

"Having more than thirty years of experience in divine healing ministry, I have observed one circumstance which I believe is the main hindrance to receiving permanent deliverance from sickness. Christians, even those who believe in divine healing, tend to accept occasional sickness and getting healed as normal, as God's order for life. But it has been made clear in the Word of God that it is not divine healing, but divine health which is God's intended plan for His children."

Please examine your own thoughts on this matter. Most likely you are like many who are in the cycle of sickness/healing, sickness/healing.

No other lifestyle will be available to you until you 'see' that this cycle was broken by His Stripes at the Cross and can be broken in your life today through faith.

EFFECTS OF EXTENDED VERBAL PRAYER
&
JOYFUL LAUGHTER

(You may not believe in glossolalia, tongues, but whatever your opinion or belief is about this subject, do not let it turn you off on the whole subject we are discussing regarding a 'life of wellness'. Tongues is not necessary to have a life of wellness. As listed below, there are a number of medically proven benefits of prayer in a heavenly language for those who have it.)

I have had a number of inquiries concerning the efficacy of praying in the spirit (glossolalia) and it's benefit to the human immune system, i.e., immunity enhanced by chemicals released from a part of the brain. I am attempting to clarify some information I have shared with a number of ministers. This is information that may be deduced from what we know about the way the brain functions. We do know the part of the brain affected most noticeably by extended prayer and laughter represents a significant portion of the brain and it's metabolic activity. Therefore, voluntary speech during extended vocal prayer causes a major stimulation in these parts of the brain (mainly the hypothalamus). The hypothalamus has direct regulation of four major systems of the body, mainly: a) the pituitary gland and all target endocrine glands; b) the total immune system; c) the entire autonomic system; and d) the production of brain hormones called endorphins and enkephalons, which are chemicals the body produces and are 100-200 times more powerful than morphine.

In summary, a very significant percentage of the central nervous system is directly and indirectly activated in the process of extended verbal and musical prayer over a period of time. This results in a significant release of brain hormones which, in turn, increases the body's general immunity. It is further enhanced through joyful laughter with increased respirations and oxygen intake to the brain, diaphragm and other muscles. This same phenomenon is seen in physical activity in general, i.e., running, etc. We know from the Word of God that there is a true joy that builds and sustains. Nehemiah tells us the joy of the Lord is our strength. There is joy in the presence of Jehovah. We, as believers having entered into that wonderful presence of our Lord, know this to be true. What we must continue to remember is that the joy of the Lord spoken of in the Word is so much more than any manifestation. We can truly have that unspeakable joy in the face of any trials we may encounter, if our joy is grounded in a knowledge of the Lord Jesus Christ. I hope the above information helps to clarify the report you received regarding my statement in the area of the physical effects of speaking in tongues and joyful laughter for extended periods of time. Truly we all benefit - body, soul, and spirit - from obedience and yielding to the Spirit of God in every area of our lives.

Carl R. Peterson, M.D.

Praying in the Spirit

Scripture commands us to "be filled with the Spirit" (Eph. 5:18). We know this means more than to "be happy", "be nice" or "act like a Christian". The Spirit of God Himself came to indwell Believers, to help and guide us (John 14:16; 16:13), teach us all things (John 14:26), show us things to come (John 16:13) and empower us (Acts 1:8).

In the Book of Acts, whenever Believers were filled with the Holy Ghost, they spoke in tongues (Acts 2:4, Acts 10:46, Acts 19:6). By the same token, when Believers in this day are filled with the Spirit, they also speak in tongues. It is my hope that we will not minimize the importance of praying in the Spirit, regardless of one's theology -- or even how it has been since one was first filled. Speaking in tongues (what the Bible sometimes calls "praying in the Spirit") edifies (energizes or charges) our spirit man (1 Cor. 14:4), builds us up (Jude 20), keeps us in the love of God (Jude 21) and give us wisdom regarding things we cannot know with by ourselves (1 Cor. 2:9-16).

Literally, when scripture tells us to "be filled with the Spirit", we are being commanded to pray in the Spirit -- to pray in tongues. Acts 5:32 says, And we are his witnesses of these things; and so is also the Holy Ghost, whom God hath given to them that obey him. In other words, staying filled with the Spirit is a matter of obedience. Most Believers who obey God in this have discovered many of the wonderful benefits of praying in the Spirit. These benefits include peace in the mind and health in the Body!

Definitions below supplied by
Mrs. Bonni Pokorny, L.P.N. of Salem, Oregon

Areas stimulated by prayer in tongues:
(I would add that these areas are also stimulated by quoting the Scripture - AW)

<u>Immune system</u>: Resistant to disease due to the development of antibodies.

<u>Pituitary gland</u>: An endocrine gland secreting a number of hormones that regulate many bodily processes including growth and reproduction, referred to as the Master Gland of the body.

<u>Autonomic system</u>: (self-controlling) Control of involuntary bodily functions. It regulates the functions of glands and the heart.

<u>Endorphins</u>: Brain hormones. These chemicals decrease pain or one's awareness of pain, thus increasing the threshold for pain.

<u>Enkephalons</u>: Same as endorphins; producing natural analgesia.

GOD DESIRES TO HEAL WITH PURPOSE

Healing, from the kingdom perspective, seeks to release the person into a full realm of destiny and purpose. Healing from God is not simply the removal of discomfort or disease only.

In many instances Jesus told those whom He healed or set free to:

"Go back home and tell what great things the Lord has done for you."

"Go show yourself to the priest"

HEALING WITHOUT DESTINY WILL BECOME A "SLOW DEATH"

Healing, without have a sense of divine destiny, will eventually become a "slow death" or empty life. Healing with destiny, becomes the beginning of an eternal flow and connection with the Father. It becomes a fresh river of Godly Creativity and Expression. Healing with destiny will change the 'normal' routine of life. It will redefine the existence of an individual, and release them into the purposes of God!

Some people seek to be healed without accepting the responsibility of purpose. They want to be freed of symptoms, but yet bound to the parameters of humanistic living.

If one's life was empty (before the sickness), the healing of God does not want the individual to return to the empty life. The Spirit will speak "fullness" into the emptiness. This is part of the healing.

To Summarize

A life of wellness **is** possible.

It is made available through the redemptive work that Jesus did *on the Cross* for you.

When He was *on earth* he demonstrated that it was God's will for people to not be sick by healing *all* who came to Him for healing.

Jesus did not act independently of the Father, so it was the Father's will in Him healing the people.

Communion illustrates the healing of your whole being…..spirit, soul and body.

Healing takes place when hands are laid upon you and the tangible presence of the Holy Spirit enters you. This power enters your spirit and from there radiates out into your body to effect healing.

You may or may not feel or sense anything. You may or may not have an immediate manifestation of healing. Obedience to the commands of Jesus, moves the power of God. Hands are laid on you in obedience to Jesus *command* to 'lay hands on the sick and they will recover'.

The only way to truly protect yourself from the attacks of the enemy (Satan), is to immerse yourself in the life and teachings of Jesus Christ. And remember that it is not enough to merely agree with those teachings, you must absorb and assimilate them.

God's goal and purpose for you while on this earth, is that your life continuously looks less like your life and more like Christ's life.

You should reach a point that allows you to walk free from the enemy's attacks, and you should also be setting the other captive's free.

Freely you have received, freely give!

The Blood Covenant

I've a right to grace, In the hardest place,
On the ground of the Blood Covenant;
I've a right to peace that can never cease,
On the ground of the Blood Covenant
I've a right to joy, that can never cloy,
On the ground of the Blood Covenant;
I've a right to power, yes, this very hour,
On the ground of the Blood Covenant,
I've a right to health, thru my Father's wealth,
On the ground of the Blood Covenant;
I, my healing take, Satan's hold must break,
On the ground of the Blood Covenant,
I've a legal right, now to win this fight,
On the ground of the Blood Covenant;
I will take my part with courageous heart,
On the ground of the Blood Covenant,
Now my rights I claim, in His Holy Name,
On the ground of the Blood Covenant;
And my prayers prevail, the all Hell assail,
On the ground of the Blood Covenant,
On the ground of the Blood,
On the ground of the Blood covenant;
I will claim my rights, though the enemy fights,
On the ground of the Blood Covenant.

Written by:
E.W. Kenyon
used with permission from
Kenyon's Gospel Publishing Society
www.kenyons.org

Further Information

www.annwindsorbibleschool.org
(location of New Life School of Pneumatology)

www.facebook.com/ann.windsor.9

https://twitter.com/pneumalady

http://www.blogtalkradio.com/zoeradionetwork

email: annwindsor8@gmail.com

For additional copies:

annwindsorpublications.blogspot.com
(inquire about multiple copy shipping discounts)

Made in United States
North Haven, CT
02 May 2023